Girl,

Don't Stop

Dreaming

Other Books by Elisa Douglas

Girl, Stop Stressing

Girl, This Is Not The End

Girl,

Don't Stop

Dreaming

Reawaken Your Dreams and Finally

Make Them Come True

By

Elisa Douglas

Awesome Wonder Books
New Jersey

Girl, Don't Stop Dreaming

TO MY MOTHER, ENID

The first woman to explain to me how important our dreams

are, and who continues to show me what it means to go after

your dreams and never give up until they come true!

Table of Contents

Introduction...2

Chapter 1: Believe in Yourself (Despite Your Fears)............10

Chapter 2: Dream BIG!...18

Chapter 3: With God and the Right Mindset......................24

Chapter 4: Trust the Process..28

Chapter 5: Stay Focused...40

Chapter 6: Have a Plan...50

Chapter 7: What Is Your Why?.......................................60

Chapter 8: Learn from the Mistakes of Others....................64

Chapter 9: Be Honest with Yourself.................................70

Chapter 10: Don't Give Up!...76

Chapter 11: It's Not Too Late!.......................................88

Conclusion 92

INTRODUCTION

Has anyone ever asked you what is your dream? What do you hope to become when you grow up? I remember being asked this question all the time as a child. My teachers asked me this question, my parents' friends asked me, and my parents would occasionally ask me this question as well. This probably happened to you a lot when you were a child as well. For me, most of the time I would just say the first thing that came to mind at the moment, and this is probably how you answered the question too.

On the other hand, maybe you answered this question based on what your parents or another of your relatives did for a living at the time. So you may have answered this question by saying, "I want to become a nurse like my mom" or "I want to become a teacher like my dad", or you may have also said that you want to become a firefighter like your uncle or a lawyer like your aunt. I am sure you get the point: You most likely said that you wanted to become what the person in your life who you admired the most did for work at the time.

Whatever answers you gave all those years ago to those people who asked you that very pertinent question, you may have stood by your answer all these years and held on to those dreams without making them a reality since you became an adult. Or you may have realized some new dreams as you got older and learnt more about different career paths. You may even have changed your mind again and again, but you just have not been able to make that dream come through yet.

A lot of times we have dreams and desires, things that we were deadest on becoming when we were children, but then we grow up and life starts taking its toll on us, and before we know it, we realize that we are much older and we still have not yet achieved our goals. Oftentimes when we realize this, we think to ourselves, "Oh, my goodness! I wanted to do this but because of my situation it never happened for me, and now it is too late for me to become what I had always dreamed of becoming. Nothing is happening for me or nothing will come to fruition right now or anytime soon. I just feel stuck, so I will have to put that dream aside because there is no point in wasting any more time and energy even thinking about it because it is just not going to happen for me."

Does this train of thought seem familiar to you? I know a lot of us tend to think like this when the going gets tough and our backs are against the wall when it comes to making our dreams come through. Of course, life gets in the way sometimes, and trust me, different situations in our lives will always make it more challenging for us to push through those barriers and continue to reach for our dreams. Maybe some of the obstacles that you have experienced so far included having a child before you planned to, or maybe you didn't have the money to go to college right after high school and you ended up not going to college at all, or maybe you never found that dream job that you always planned to get after college.

Regardless of what your dream was, that driving force in your life, it was put on the backburner and before you knew it, you had a family to take care of and no time to focus on your dream. You know, you find that perfect partner and you start having babies and then you get so immersed in your family life, so much so that you focus only on your family and you put your own dreams on hold for the time being, and of course, you keep telling yourself that this is not forever, it is only for the time being.

Now, this is your dream we are talking about here, so, of course, you felt so strongly about it for such a long time that it almost felt like your first child, that first thing that you thought about constantly, that you kept in your heart and nurtured, because it was so important to you and it gave you so much hope for the future. So even though that dream was put on the backburner in your life, it never really left your mind, and you still find yourself thinking about it sometimes.

However, because you have to take care of your family, you forgot all about yourself in the process. For instance, you may need to be available when your children get home from school in the evenings so you can take them to soccer or cheerleading practice, or you may the only ones who clean and cook at your house, or you may even have to help your husband with his business sometimes, or you may be needed by the members of your family to take care of a whole host of other things, based on your own situation.

You forget that you also have wants and needs, and you also had a dream that used to consume your mind so completely that you were determined to see it come true. This is so very often the case with us women. We often forget about ourselves: we forget that we used to have hopes; that we used to have goals; that we used to have dreams; and that there were things that we had planned to do with our lives for our personal satisfaction and sense of accomplishment when we were younger.

Those dreams were pushed aside for years and years and you may now think that it is too late for you to see them come true, for you to finally (yes, FINALLY!) see that dream become a reality. But is it really too late for you? Should you really give up on what you had hoped to do or become in life simply because you didn't accomplish those things at an earlier age? Now, let's really dive into this topic so we can reconnect with ourselves and revive those precious dreams!

However, let us first examine the concept of a dream in this context. So, what is a dream? A dream is really anything that we hope for; anything that we aspire to do or to become in life. It is something that may seem unreal when it is first conceived, like it can never come to fruition. Regardless of how unlikely it may seem that your dream will one day become your reality, you still dream it, because it is a dream and, more importantly, it is your dream! It is something that you think about all the time, and something that your heart yearns for, relentlessly.

Unlike the dreams that we have when we go to sleep at nights, which is often a series of thoughts or images or even sensations, this dream that I am talking about is something that we all have inside of us. It is a cherished aspiration or ambition; it is something that we wish and hope and pray for. Sometimes we don't even really believe our dreams ourselves, and we may wonder if we are out of our minds for dreaming something that is so wild and so far 'out there', because we can't really see it ever becoming a reality, but we have a fervent

hope and desire that it will come true- one day, someday, in fact,

just about any day- before we leave this earth.

Elisa Douglas

CHAPTER 1

Believe in Yourself (Despite Your Fears)

Nothing affects whether or not our dreams come true more than our belief in ourselves to actually make them come true. Your belief in yourself is the extent to which you think you have what it takes to achieve your goals. It is the amount of confidence you have in your own abilities and the amount of fire you have in your belly to make your dreams come true. The extent to which we believe in ourselves is often affected by our social upbringing, our self-esteem, and the amount of success we have already experienced in life.

Even when we doubt our own abilities to actually make our dreams become our reality, it is crucial that we have the right mindset and believe in ourselves just enough to not actually give up on those dreams. It is imperative to our peace of minds and to our overall health that we keep those dreams alive! We must continue to reach for our dreams at all costs, whatever it takes, whatever we have to do to make them happen. In the introduction, I spoke about how we sometimes forget about our dreams, those things that we had hoped to become when we grow up. However, because of circumstances beyond your control, you may have settled for something that was less than what you had hoped to become, and you opted to lower the bar that you had set for yourself in regards to reaching out and grabbing your dreams with both hands.

You may have dreamt of becoming a doctor or lawyer, or of having a similar career where you must first get a bachelor's degree before you can apply to go to school to study for that specific career choice. However, because your family could not afford it, you were not able to go to college at all. The lack of money got in the way and became a major problem and you started to think that your dream had been too far-fetched anyway, that you had set the bar way too high for you to reach it. If this is your situation, I implore you to stop that train of thought immediately! Think about all the options that you have available and go make your dream come true. There may even be more than one answer to your problem. The answer may be scholarships, grants, student loans, private loans, using credit cards, or a combination of any of these possible solutions. Or you may even be able to find other solutions to this financial problem, but whatever solution you come up with, you have to be relentless and resilient. Your dream can come true if you are determined enough to make it happen.

You have to push away those beliefs that tell you that there are limits to the things that you can do and how much you can accomplish. Get rid of the lack of confidence by constantly giving yourself pep talks each and every day and, most importantly, you must stare at your fear, acknowledge it, but push through it anyway. We all have fears, and when we set out to make our dreams come true, our fear of the unknown, that fear of taking a new journey toward our dreams, will always try to stay at the forefront and will try to keep us from moving forward. The fear will try to overpower all our other emotions. It will grip us and try to keep us in its stronghold. It can paralyze us to the extent where we feel numb and unable to move forward toward our dreams.

No one who has ever accomplished anything that they truly value did so without feeling fear. However, they pushed through those fears, they looked their fears right in the eye, so to speak, and continued on their path to success, despite those fears. Fear is an emotion that comes quite easily and naturally to all humans. Fear alerts us to the presence of danger or the threat of harm, whether that threat is real or imagined. We all experience fear at different times in our lives, especially when we move out of our comfort zones and are facing the unknown. How we deal with our fear when it rears its ugly head is what makes the difference between successful people and those who are unsuccessful in achieving their goals.

It is therefore natural that we will experience fear when we decide to go after our dreams. When we start taking steps toward the things we want to achieve in life, we are moving beyond the things that we are familiar and thereby comfortable with into unfamiliar territory. As such, fear will show up when we are moving beyond our normal routine and way of life to an unknown place with new experiences, but we cannot allow our fear to get the best of us and keep us from living our dreams. If we allow our fears to keep us paralyzed from going after our dreams, then they will remain as dreams forever and we will never get to experience them in reality because all we will be left with are constant thoughts of what our lives would be like if only we had decided to push through those fears.

Whenever you are going after your dreams and you start experiencing fear, acknowledge that it is there but make a conscious decision to push through it so you can keep moving forward. Think about all that you are likely to lose if you let your fear get the best of you. Ask yourself if it will be better for you to stay in your comfort zone and continue to dream about your dreams and the life you want for yourself, or if pursuing your dreams is worth the risk of pushing past your fear and going out of your comfort zone to an unknown journey toward your dreams. Always keep in mind that getting rid of your fear by staying in your comfort zone will leave you in your current position where you are not living the life that you want for yourself. You will be giving up your dreams because of your fear.

When you truly believe in yourself, here's what happens: You choose to give yourself the things that you need; you embrace the things that seem impossible so that you can make them become possible; you keep going toward your dreams regardless of the failures and obstacles that come in your path, no matter what; you trust your own judgment and listen to your inner voice; you work with purpose based on your goals and you refrain from doing things that are meaningless and will not help you to achieve your goals; you do not second-guess your decisions or hesitate when opportunities come your way, you just go for it; you remain fully committed to achieving your goals and your belief in yourself never wavers; you stay focused on why you want to accomplish your dreams to keep you motivated and; you keep up your momentum by constantly taking small steps toward your goals. Remember, even the small steps are important because they too play a big part in whether or not you will accomplish your dreams.

To make your dreams become a reality, you have to believe in yourself, you have to believe that you have what it takes to make it happen. You have to believe that no matter what everyone else says, no matter how much others try to discourage you from reaching for your goals, if you stay on your path to success, you can achieve those goals. Do not allow yourself to get distracted or to be dissuaded from your true purpose.

When you do not have the support of your relatives and friends when you are trying to accomplish your dreams, you still have to believe in yourself and do what you need to do to prove them wrong. Show them that you could make your dreams become your reality despite their discouragement and without their support. How hungry are you for that dream? How badly do you want it? If you truly believe in yourself, by your actions alone you can tell people, "I don't need your extrinsic motivation right now. I have enough intrinsic motivation inside of me that God put in my heart to help me achieve my goals. I believe in myself so I know that I can make this happen for myself because it will give me the personal satisfaction that I need to be happy with myself. I will make my dreams become my reality, even if you choose not to stand by me."

Push the naysayers out of your mind! Be persistent and remain focused, even when there are so many stumbling blocks in your way that everyone else tells you to quit and just give it up! You cannot afford to let go of your dreams without first giving it your best shot. To make your dreams become a reality, you have to be prepared for the fight of your life! If you tell yourself that this is what you truly want and you keep your eyes on that dream, trust and believe when I say that you can make it happen. Every morning, look yourself in the mirror and repeat these words, "I believe in myself! I know I can do it! I know that I have what it takes to do it! I will not allow anyone or anything to stop me from going after my dreams. I will keep going until my dreams come true!" You got this, girl! You can do it!

CHAPTER 2

Dream BIG!

Have you every shared your dreams with someone before, only for that person to tell you that your dream is too big? That you should stop being ridiculous and get a more realistic dream? That you should get your head out of the clouds and back to earth because you will never be able to make that dream become a reality? Personally, I don't think that it is possible for anyone to dream too big.

It is very important that you dream big. When you dream big, you start seeing the possibility of things that looked improbable or maybe even impossible to you before. It is crucial to remain steadfast when it comes to reaching for your dreams. When you first conceive your dream, you may not be able to see it happening for you at all, but it is vital to your success that you remain committed to seeing your dreams become your reality. If you can think it, believe me, it is possible. However, you have to want your dream badly enough to keep going when the going gets tough. You have to envision what your life will be like when you finally accomplish that dream. You have to imagine how much better things will be for you and the ways in which your life (and maybe even that of family members) will change for the better when those dreams finally come true. If you are not hungry enough for your dreams to become a reality, you will never be able to see the changes those dreams can make to your life and you will never be able to envision what your life will be like once those dreams come true. You have to want your dream badly enough before you will get the grit you will need to make it happen!

You should want your dream so badly that you actually dream about it whenever you go to sleep. Your dreams can be as big as you want them to be; they can be as ridiculous and unrealistic as everyone else thinks they are. You should not focus on what other people have to say about your dreams, because they are yours, not anyone else's. You have to remain strong and disciplined, persistent and committed in order to achieve your dreams. The psychologist, Carl Maslow, spoke about intrinsic and extrinsic motivation, both of which can be powerful sources of motivation for anyone. However, in my opinion, intrinsic motivation is the most powerful type of motivation that there is. With extrinsic motivation, your behaviors are stimulated by external factors whereby you receive motivation from others because you want to earn a reward or avoid some type of punishment.

On the other hand, intrinsic motivation is driven by a deep internal desire for personal fulfillment or satisfaction, and this desire serves as a catalyst for your behavior. In other words, intrinsic motivation occurs when you are motivated by your personal desire to achieve something that will be rewarding to you personally. Intrinsic motivation is more powerful than extrinsic motivation because the desire that we each have inside of us to achieve our goals is what drives us to seek a more rewarding and fulfilling life. Intrinsic motivation is the source of excitement that pushes us to follow our dreams and to do what we truly desire to do with our lives.

The desire inside of us to do more, to become more, to reach for greater heights, to be the best versions of ourselves, is the driving force behind our success and accomplishments.

So now you may be thinking, "Well, Elisa, what if my dream is to have a house that has 20 bedrooms and 30 bathrooms. Are you saying that this dream would not be unrealistic?" Well, a dream like this can be looked at from several different angles. One problem you may encounter is finding a builder who is actually able to build such a huge residential property. You may also have problems finding a piece of land that is big enough for a house that size or getting permits to start building in the town of your choice. In this case, you may have to do some research to find somewhere else where you would be able to get a permit to build a residential property of that size.

You may even have to look outside of your country for the piece of land that will be ideal for your dream house. When we have big dreams, we may have to change our plans several times along the way to see them become a reality, but if we persist and are flexible, they can certainly happen. They may not come true in a year or two, or even in five or ten years, but if you keep going and working toward those dreams, they will eventually come true.

When your dream is bigger than what other people expect or think your dream should be, there is an even greater feeling of satisfaction that comes from seeing those dreams come true. This is because the achievement of those dreams can serve as validation that you were correct in listening to your heart and following the path that you felt compelled to stay on. You are sure to feel such a deep sense of joy, peace and fulfillment that you will become much more confident because you will know that all the stress that you went through to get to that point in your life where you actually accomplished your dreams were well worth it.

Dream big and be persistent in following your dreams. I promise you: it will not be a waste of your time. You shouldn't just aim to reach for the stars: you should aim to reach beyond the stars to accomplish your dreams. Do not listen to the naysayers in your life; remove the negativity out of your head because when they tell you that your dreams will never come true, they are talking nonsense! That is so not true! Giving up should never be an option when it comes to your dreams, but you have to remember that no one is going to make your dreams happen for you; you have to go out there and make them happen for yourself!

Your dreams can never be too big! This is why dreams are called just that: DREAMS! The whole point of dreams is for them to initially appear to be something that is far-fetched and unreal, something we can only dream about but will likely never truly see them become our reality. Your dream should be huge, gigantic, something you cannot even wrap your head around when it is first conceived. Your dreams are about reaching beyond the stars. It is about massive goals and humongous thoughts! However, to make those massive goals and thoughts become a reality, you have to take massive action, but massive action will be worth it only if you truly trust the process, which will be discussed in further detail in chapter 4.

CHAPTER 3

With God and the Right Mindset

Having the right mindset is crucial when it comes to realizing your dreams. Even more importantly, though, is knowing God and believing in Him as a power that is greater than yourself. Whether you call Him God, Jesus, Yahweh, Jehovah, or anything else, believing and trusting in a higher power, someone or something that is bigger, greater and more powerful than anything or anyone else on earth, is vital to us accomplishing our dreams.

When you believe in a higher power, you will feel strengthened and confident as you reach for your goals because you will know that there is someone that you can always call on for help in times of distress, frustration and grief. Knowing that this spirit or person is watching over you, guiding and protecting you, will give you the confidence to keep going for your dreams even when you face disappointments and stumbling blocks along the way.

Continue to hang in there and put your trust in God because He can move all mountains and literally shelter you from the storms that will likely come your way from time to time. You will definitely not have the strength that you will need to see your dreams truly come to fruition by yourself. Without God, you will not have that higher power to call upon when you cannot handle the pressures that comes with reaching for your dreams. You will feel down and broken during times of hardship and despair. In times like these, you will feel that it is just too much for you to bear alone and these are often the times when we throw in the towel and give up on our dreams.

However, when you are aware that there is a higher power that you can call upon, you will realize that you have someone to help you get through those rough patches on your way to accomplishing your dreams. Pray to God, call upon His name, trust Him with your problems, with your wants and needs, and with the challenges you are facing. Invite Him to intervene on your behalf and to fix those problems and to help you get through them unscathed. Ask Him to guide you along the path toward your dreams. Ask Him for the strength, courage, determination, and the right mindset that you will need to accomplish your dreams.

What is mindset? Mindset is a frame of mind. It is a collection of thoughts and beliefs that shape how people think and the actions that ultimately result from those thoughts. It is a set of methods or assumptions that are held by a person or group of people. It is often influenced by how a person view the world or of that person's philosophy of life. Mindset can be a powerful incentive that can cause a person to continue to behave in a particular way or make certain choices. However, a positive mindset that is strong is a critical part of having a healthy self-esteem. Mindset can also help to reinforce our most private feelings and beliefs about themselves. It determines how a person interprets and deals with different situations.

Without the right mindset, it is highly unlikely that you will push yourself long and hard enough to make your dreams come true. You will find that you give up too quickly and easily before giving yourself the opportunity to truly grow and reach your full potential. It is very important that you put yourself in the frame of mind where you think of yourself as already successful. As I mentioned chapter, while you sleep, you should dream about living your dreams. You should be purposeful in everything that you do. Focus only on the positives, and do not allow yourself to be influenced by the negativity that will likely be all around you. Stay true to who you are and continue to believe in yourself; believe that you have what it takes to make your dreams come true. In everything that you attempt to do, you will accomplish those things only if you have the right mindset. My mantra has always been and will continue to be: You can do anything that you put your mind to!

You have to trust the process though, so now let's get into chapter 4, where we will talk more about trusting the process, which involves the steps that you will be required to take when you are trying to accomplish your dreams.

CHAPTER 4

Trust the Process

When it comes to following our dreams, there is a process that we all have to follow to successfully accomplish those dreams. Of course, the process may look different from one person to the next because we have different goals, and so the road we take to achieve them will be different.

First, remember that nothing at all happens before its time. If it is not the time for something to happen, that thing will just not happen, regardless of how you feel about it; regardless of how badly you want that thing to happen based on your timeline. Ecclesiastics 3:1 (KJV) reads, "To every thing there is a season, and a time to every purpose under the heaven." This means that there is a time and a purpose for everything on earth. Just like we have distinguished weather patterns and temperatures for the different seasons in a year, so there is a season for different things to occur in our lives as well.

There is a time when we are happy and a time when we are sad. A time when we feel like things are going well in our lives and a time when we feel like everything is going bad for us and we just can't get a break.

This is also true when we are trying to make our dreams come true. There will be stumbling blocks along the way, but sometimes things will go smoothly, and you may find that you are able to cover a lot of ground in a short amount of time on your way to making your dreams become your reality and your new way of life. In other words, making our dreams come true is a process that involves a number of steps even though the steps you will need to take may differ based on what your dreams are.

Regardless of what your dreams are, there will be a series of steps that you must take to achieve your goals and see your greatest desires fulfilled. While there is usually no way to cut through these steps and go straight from point A to point Z (even if you have some serious cash lying around, nothing but time on your hands and luck is totally on your side), there are a few things you can do to eliminate some of the steps.

The steps to realizing one's dream include conception of the idea or goal for your dream, taking the first step toward that dream, facing the inevitable challenges, setbacks, changes in your situation, taking wrong turns or making mistakes, putting your dreams on hold or making minor or major changes to your dream, re-focusing your priorities, getting back on the path to your success, staying focused, persistent and resilient, and finally, seeing your dreams come true. While some people may be fortunate enough to skip some of these steps on their way to making their dreams come true, most of us will experience all of them.

One thing that you can do to eliminate at least one of the steps to accomplishing your dreams is to learn from the mistakes of others. In chapter 8, I will discuss why it is so important that we learn from the mistakes of others when we are reaching for our dreams. Not only will learning from the mistake of others eliminate some of the steps that you would otherwise have to take on the path to accomplishing your dreams, but it will also save you a lot of time, energy and money. Another way that you can eliminate some of the steps when trying to accomplish your dreams is to have a solid written plan of action that you stick to and follow to the letter. In chapter 6, I will discuss the big part that a comprehensive written plan plays in whether or not we accomplish our dreams, despite the amount of effort that we put into it.

Another way to eliminate some of the steps to making your dreams come true is to build a network of people who care about you and who truly want to see you succeed. These are the people in your life who will continuously lift you up and support you always, no matter what. When you have people who you love and trust in your corner and they feel the same way about you, they will always be looking out for your best interests, so they will do research on your behalf and do whatever else is necessary to help push you up the ladder toward your dreams. Having people who you can count on will always make the strain of going after your dreams that much easier to get through because you will know that you are not alone.

Girl, Don't Stop Dreaming

You will know that there are people by your side to pull you up when you're feeling down. They will be there to help motivate you so that you don't give up even when your intrinsic motivation, the drive that exists inside of you, is not enough to keep you going. If you do not have to, don't go it alone. Let your loved ones know of your plan so they can help you get to our dreams. They will also be there to hold you accountable when you are slacking off and starts to deviate from your plan.

Since there is a time and a season for everything, it is important to remember that things will happen for you only when they are meant to happen, that is, only when it is time for them to happen. We have to keep trusting the process that is necessary for us to accomplish our dreams, even when things are not progressing as much as we want them to or are not moving in the direction that we expected them to go. When we are on the path toward our dreams, we have to be prepared for the setbacks that will inevitably occur, and for this reason, it is important that you have a written plan that you follow because you will know exactly what to do when those setbacks occur. Of course, we should always hope for the best, but expecting setbacks and having a plan in place regarding how we will deal with them is also important.

Regardless of the setbacks that you experience as you reach for your dreams, you have to continue to believe in yourself and trust that the setbacks are a part of the process, but you should also remain persistent because you truly believe that you have it takes to keep going forward until you get to the finish line. This finish line is where you will find your dream lying in wait of you to claim them as yours, as you will have every right to do, at that point. Regardless of the number of stumbling blocks that you will face, you simply cannot give up because if you do, you will feel regret and you will constantly wonder if you could have done it, if you could have made your dreams come true had you only stayed the course for a little while longer. Anything that is worthwhile will not come easy. If it was easy to accomplish our dreams then, quite frankly, they would not be dreams. Our dreams would become a part of our normal, everyday routine instead of something that we have to work long and hard to accomplish.

It is also imperative that you celebrate each progress that you make toward your dreams. There will be little wins and big wins, and it is important that you celebrate them all. Do something fun that makes you happy in celebration each time you take another step in the direction toward your dreams. Celebrate with your family and friends and allow them to congratulate you on both the big steps and the little ones. Any progress that you make when following your dreams is worth celebrating because this will help you to stay motivated and focused on where you are in the process.

The road to fulfilling your dreams will always be covered with both opportunities and challenges. Both the opportunities and the challenges are a part of the process to making your dreams come true. It is therefore vital to your success that you trust both sides of the coin, that is, both the opportunities and the challenges. For example, if you want to become a nanny because you absolutely love children and that is really what you want to do as a career, that is absolutely fine, but do not think that it will come without its own set of challenges.

As far as I know, many families do not require their nannies to have a specific educational background, and so you may start applying to jobs after high school without having any qualifications or work experience that is related to a job as a nanny. However, for the first few jobs that you apply to, the families may judge you because you have no children of your own, or because you do not have any prior experience as a nanny. They may also judge you based on your age, your physical appearance or mannerisms, or any other number of things.

All of these are challenges that could result in you not getting a job as a nanny for a long time. In this case, the best route of action to take would be to continue to apply to nanny positions and 'keep you head up', so to speak. If you find yourself in this situation, it would be crucial that you start connecting with people from a variety of backgrounds and age ranges on a personal level and then you may either be able to get a referral from someone or you may become friends with a family who eventually becomes your employer. As I mentioned earlier, it is important that you build a network of people who will support you and help to steer you in the right direction when you are trying to make your dreams come true.

On the other hand, you may find yourself on the other end of the spectrum where you start applying to different nanny positions and you start receiving job offers right away, for one reason or another. Maybe it is because of your personality, your maturity, your trustworthiness, or they may test you by allowing you to spend some time with their children and then they may realize that you are extremely good with children because you may be a natural nurturer and children easily gravitate toward you. In this case, you would have many opportunities available to you and so you would need to accept the offer that you feel would be the best one for you. You may even have the opportunity to negotiate your salary and time off, or you may want to select the family who you have the strongest connection with or who you feel most comfortable with.

However, if your dream is to become a heart surgeon, you will experience very different opportunities and challenges than those that are experienced by someone who wants to become a nanny. First, you may not have the financial means necessary to study continuously after high school to accomplish your dream and so you may first have to find a job even before you start college. Some people start college but have to work one or more jobs during those four years in an effort to pay for their expenses.

These challenges may further be compounded by your need to volunteer at a medical office to gain experience that will make it easier to get into medical school. After college, you may then encounter more stumbling blocks, either in the way of the Medical College Admission Test (MCAT) which all applicants to medical schools in the U.S. are required to take, or it may be getting accepted into a medical school, or finding the money to go to medical school.

After overcoming all these obstacles and finishing those four years of medical school, you still have to continue your studies for a few more years to specialize in heart surgery. There may be opportunities along the way though, in the form of grants and scholarships, parents and other family members who are there to support, encourage, motivate and uplift you, or getting accepted by a whole slew of medical schools and having the tough but wonderful opportunity to decide which medical school you should attend.

The road to all our dreams is a series of steps and processes. It is important to understand and accept this fact so that you are prepared, mentally, physically and emotionally, to trust the process and believe that you will come out on the other side living your dreams and enjoying life to the fullest because you stayed the course and you did what you had to do to make your dreams come true. The feeling of satisfaction and fulfillment that comes with accomplishing our dreams make the long, curvy and challenging road to get there all worth it. Many sacrifices will have to be made, and in most cases, blood (hopefully, not literally), sweat and tears will have to be shed, but in the end, it will be all worth it!

Your dreams can be either big or small. It is all up to you and your goals for your life. I don't believe that there is any such thing as a dream that is too big or one that is too small. It is your dream, so people can judge all they want. That shouldn't stop you at all. Keep pushing forward so that you can live the life you want because only then will you be truly happy and contented with your life as it is.

CHAPTER 5

Stay Focused

In this chapter, we will discuss the importance of staying focused: knowing what you want and keeping your eyes on accomplishing your dreams. While you can get away with putting your dreams on hold for a while, you cannot afford to get sidetracked indefinitely, or you will never see your dreams come true. You may have to watch others who had similar dreams live their best lives by accomplishing those dreams, but you will not get to live those dreams yourself. This is why you must stay focused when it comes to your dreams.

Seeing your dreams come true is often a long-fought battle and a reward that is well-deserved, but you have to go after that prize and claim it as your own. Do not wait for anyone to come and give it to you because, trust me, you will be waiting forever for that to happen. Of course, no one is going to just walk up to you and hand you your dreams on a silver platter. I wish (and probably you do too) that life was that easy, but the fact of the matter is that it isn't that easy, no, not by a long shot! Since accomplishing our dreams is not as easy as we would want it to be, we have to remain really focused on the prize at the end of the tunnel, which is, of course, actually living our dreams. You have to go out there and grab your dream for yourself. You have to work extremely hard and you have to be tenacious if you are going to get there. You have to want it badly enough that you feel a deep hunger when you think about your dream. You should be like a starving woman when it comes to your dream.

Your dream should be like the sustenance that your mind, body and soul need to keep them alive, to keep them going strong; the sustenance that you need to feel happy, fulfilled and at peace. To make your dream become your reality, you have to stay extremely focused. You cannot allow yourself to get distracted to the extent that you divert from your path to accomplishing your dreams. To achieve your goals, you have to stay on the path to make it happen for yourself. It is about having structure on your path and being fully committed to staying the course and standing the test of time even when your dream is taking much longer to come true than you had anticipated.

I want to share with you a story about my mom and her journey to making her dreams come true. This story is about how she stood the test of time, stayed the course and remained resilient in the face of challenges because she was determined to make her dreams come true, no matter what. At the age of eight years old, my mom decided that she wanted to become a nurse. She said that she went to a hospital for the very first time at that age and she saw the nurses in their white uniforms. As she recalls it, to her, those nurses looked very important, they looked very focused, they looked like true professionals with a meaningful purpose, and she was intrigued by them and the work they were doing. She said that it was right then and there that she decided that she also wanted to become a nurse when she grew up.

My mom remained steadfast with this decision as she got older. She became more confident that this was the right career choice for her after she read and learnt all she could about the nursing profession. However, she encountered one stumbling block after another on her way to making this dream of hers come true. Immediately after graduating from high school, with her qualifications in hand, my mom started applying to nursing school. She was raised in Jamaica and at the time, there was only one nursing school on the island and it was government owned. As such, people who wanted to get into the program had to apply and wait until they got through.

While a lot of people got into the program the first time they applied, this was not the case for my mother who had to apply repeatedly. In fact, each letter of response she received from the school informed her that she had not been accepted into the program to start training with the newest batch of students, but that she should re-apply in eighteen months. This was the response she received for several years, but she continued to apply to the program after every eighteen months as instructed, because she was determined to make her dream come true, no matter how long it would take.

She did not give up and remained focused because nursing was what she was 100% sure that she wanted to do as a career for the rest of her life. She followed the instructions she was given in those letters and continued to apply and re-apply to the program but, in the meantime, she knew she had to do something else for work because she had to keep herself occupied while she waited to get into the program. As such, she learnt how to sew and started making clothes for children in her community, then she started a preschool and was able to make the uniforms for her students. My grandmother was a post mistress at the time, and so my mom would also help my grandma with her work at the post office when she had the time to do so.

Despite all of these other jobs that she kept doing while she waited patiently to get into nursing school, my mother never once lost sight of her dream of becoming a nurse. She simply decided to learn and utilize other important skills in the interim so she could earn a living and have those skills to fall back on if necessary, in the future, but she kept her focus on her dream. She continued to apply to the nursing program over and over and over again until she finally got into the program when she was 26 years old. My mom therefore had to wait for almost eight years until she was accepted into nursing school, which was her only path to making her dream of becoming a nurse a reality at the time, since formal training is mandatory for this career.

A lot of people would have given up and thrown in the towel years before my mom was finally accepted into the nursing program. They would have chosen not to stay the course and stand the test of time because they would not have had the patience necessary. They would not have wanted that dream badly enough to remain focused on making it happen. They would not have been hungry enough for that dream, so they would have lost focus and probably would have decided to settle for remaining a seamstress or a pre-school owner even though neither of those career choices had really been their dream.

A lot of people would have thought, "This is too much, it is too stressful, they keep rejecting my application and keep denying me entry into the program. They will never accept me, so why should I continue to waste my time by applying? This is torture, and I am just needlessly punishing myself by continuing to apply every eighteen months." However, my mom did not see the situation like that at all. She told herself that she really wanted to become a nurse, and she was determined that she would become one, regardless of how long it would take. She also knew that she was qualified for the program, and so she refused to give up, even as she sharpened her skills in other areas.

This was her thought on the matter: "I refuse to give up until they accept me into the program. They are going to get so tired of seeing an application with my name on it and they will realize that I will not give up, so sooner or later, they will decide to let me into the program." And that is exactly what my mom did. She continued to apply until she got into the program. My mom had a very, very successful career as a midwife and she absolutely loved it! Over the course of her career which spanned almost 40 years, she received numerous awards from the Jamaican government for her diligent service and commitment, and for her significant contribution to the nursing profession in the country. She is considered a local hero and her name is proudly displayed in bold letters in her honor at the Healthcare Center where she worked for many, many years.

If my mom had decided to give up on her dreams all those years ago when her applications to the nursing school were repeatedly rejected, she would have missed out on a very fulfilling and rewarding career. Her life would have turned out much differently than it did, and she would not have impacted the thousands of lives that she has or be an inspiration to so many people today. She would have lost the opportunity to deliver thousands of babies safely into the arms of their mothers and would not have experienced the successful and rewarding career that she has enjoyed all these years.

I am very proud of my mother for her diligence, her persistence, her tenacity, her faith and her unwavering focus on her dream. She chose to remain focused on her passion because she was certain that she could make the most impact on people's lives by serving as a nurse. Her refusal to get sidetracked and her motivation have inspired my siblings and I to also follow our dreams and to not give up until those dreams become our reality. She taught us that if we remain focused and trust the process by being patient, have the right mindset and trust in God, that we can make our dreams come true too.

Whatever your dreams are, whatever is your passion, whatever it is that you want to become in life, it will not come easy and may take much longer to happen than you had expected it to, but you have to stay the course and keep working hard toward that dream and it will eventually come true, if you believe in yourself enough and refuse to give up.

You have to really stay focused; you have to be steadfast; you cannot look at the stumbling blocks in your way and decide that they are too much to overcome and tell yourself that there is no way for you to get past them. I hope that my mom's journey to making her dream come true will also inspire you to go after your dreams regardless of the setbacks that you may encounter along the way, that you will not give up on your dreams and decide to live a subpar life instead of reaching your full potential. I hope her story will inspire you to do whatever it is that will make you happy and feel contented with your life. I hope that you will keep pushing yourself until you achieve your goals and start living your dream. Come on ladies, let's go get it!

CHAPTER 6

Have A Plan

Whatever your dreams are, whatever your goals are for the future, whatever you aspire to become in life, you need to have a plan. Whether your dream is to become a mother or a wife, whether it is to become a best-selling author, whether it is to complete a 5K marathon, whether it is to be named teacher of the year in your school district, whatever your dream is, you need to have a written plan that you will use as your guide to make that dream come true. When you put whatever you want to do or to become on paper, that dream will immediately become much more possible.

A lot of people talk about vision boards and many people make their vision boards at the end of each year for the following year or they may wait until the beginning of each new year to create their vision boards for that year. People do this so that they will have a constant visual reminder of the goals they have set for themselves for any given year and what they want to accomplish over the course of that year.

Of course, the vision boards of no two people will look exactly the same because we all have different goals that we set for ourselves. We all have different things that we want to accomplish in any given year and those things are your goals for that year. Your goals for any given year will likely have to do with your career and finances, home life, travel, health, relationships, and/or personal growth, which may include your social life, furthering your education or even your spirituality. Some people may want to travel the world or travel to a particular country in a given year, while other people may want to build their dream home or buy their dream car during that year. Others may want to start a family or go back to school or get that dream job that they have been hoping to get for years.

Your written plan should be a layout of how you will accomplish your dreams. The plan should consist of a series of steps indicating how you will get from point A (when you first decided what your dream was) to point Z (accomplishing your dream and finally living your best life). Having a plan as a guide to follow along the way, and the path to take when you come across stumbling blocks or when you receive multiple opportunities on your way up the ladder toward your dreams, will help you get there much sooner than you would have without a written plan.

A plan of action will make it much easier for you to stay on track. It is important to review your plan of action either before bed each night or shortly after you wake up each morning (or you can review your plan both morning and night), so that you will be constantly reminded of what you want to accomplish. You will also feel more focused and confident as you move forward toward your dreams because you will have that plan of action as your guide.

Your plan should have a series of steps highlighting how you will achieve your goals, so put pen to paper and write down how exactly you plan to accomplish your dreams. Your written plan should include all potential opportunities and challenges that you think may come your way as you move toward fulfilling your dreams, and how you will deal with those opportunities and overcome those challenges. It is also important for you to have a timeline of when each step in your plan will happen. Each step may not necessarily happen based on your timeline because there will be opportunities and challenges occurring that you did not anticipate at all. However, when you have a timeline for reaching a goal, you are more likely than not to reach that goal in the timeline that you gave yourself to achieve it.

If you have a group of people in your corner who are there to support and uplift you on your journey toward your dreams, ask them for help in putting your plan of action together because they too will want what is best for you and they may foresee opportunities and challenges or steps that you will need to take to get to your dreams that you may not able to see for yourself. It is important that we are honest with ourselves while we are on this unknown journey toward our dreams and that we ask for help when necessary. While you should not be afraid to ask for help when you need it, you should also be willing to accept help from others when it is offered. I will discuss the importance of being honest with ourselves in chapter 9.

As I previously mentioned, your written plan of action to accomplish your dreams should include a list of the specific steps that you will need to take to accomplish your dreams. You should be very specific about what it is you want to achieve. Write down your goal and set a deadline when you intend to accomplish each of them. The steps that you may need to take toward your goals may include applying for jobs, studying, taking a course, or developing the required skills in other ways. Do not be passive; you must start acting on your plan as soon as it is written. Passivity does not help when you are trying to accomplish your dream, so you must start taking action right away and be consistent with the amount of work you put into accomplishing that dream.

Educate yourself about your dream by reading a lot and listening to the advice of others, especially those who have walked in your shoes and have already accomplished the dream that you are trying to make happen for yourself. However, think carefully about each advice you are given and listen to your gut before you decide whether or not you will follow those pieces of advice.

Examine your goals often and do not be afraid or ashamed to remove any that may no longer apply to you for one reason or another, such as your circumstances changing. Your dream may also change over time because you may have decided to go in a different direction with your life. During the process of reaching your dreams, it is important that you stay true to who you are at all times. Develop the skills that you will need to propel your dreams forward, whether it is taking a necessary course, volunteering at a related company to learn more about what it will be like to live your dream, etcetera. Take the first step toward reaching your dream and do not stop until you have accomplished that dream.

Throughout the process, reinforce positive affirmations by telling yourself that you have already accomplished your dreams. This will help you develop the right mindset that you will need to make it to the end without faltering. When you do this, your subconscious mind will accept your dream and you will be even more motivated to accomplish it because this will keep you excited and aware of that dream that is lying on the horizon. Visualizing your dreams and imaging the life you will live after you have accomplished them will also do wonders for your subconscious mind, which will subsequently increase your intrinsic motivation to accomplish those dreams.

Take advantage of new ideas and opportunities that are presented to you on your way to accomplishing your dreams, but always follow your intuition when doing so. After you accomplish your dream, you should reward yourself by living your best life, yes, the life you have always dreamed of living! After you have put in the hard work and accomplish your dreams, you should then relax and enjoy the fruits of your labor, after all, you will have earned it!

If you write your long- and short-term goals down on paper or in a journal and you read those goals daily, you will constantly remind yourself of what your goals are and this frequent reminder will result in you being much more likely to achieve those goals. Being constantly reminded of your goals will serve as a powerful source of motivation and you will be inspired to make them become a reality. If you follow these steps, your goals will seem much more attainable and you will be more motivated to work even harder to achieve them. I also suggest that you create an alternative plan to accomplish your dreams in the event that the first plan you implemented to get you from point A to point Z does not work.

In addition to having a written plan of action that outlines how you will accomplish your dream, I also recommend that you create a vision board which will indicate how you imagine your life will look like when you are living your dream. This visual reminder will serve as a concrete representation of your aspirations and desires for a fulfilling and satisfying life. When you look at that board and remind yourself of the life that you want to live, you will be compelled and inspired to continue to pursue your dreams, your most important life goals, and to make everything on that vision board become your reality. The vision board of your dreams should be posted somewhere where you can see it every single day. The perfect place for you may be your bedroom or your home office, or anywhere else where you cannot avoid seeing it every day. You will be constantly reminded of the rewards that will likely come your way if you stay focused and follow your dreams.

Business owners have business plans that they follow to the letter because they know that that business plan is what they will use to get from point A to point B to point C and so on until they get to point Z in their businesses. In this case, point Z will most likely never be accomplished because there will always be room for improvement and room to do better, to expand more. The goals of a business have a lot to do with constant growth, expansion and scaling, so in most cases, business owners are constantly looking for new ideas and opportunities to grow and reach that next level in their businesses. This next level for business owners may include opening more stores, increasing their online presence, adding another service area to their portfolio, or any other number of expansion and improvement ideas to better serve their target customers and make more money.

However, when you are an individual writing a plan regarding how you will go about reaching your goals and making your dreams come true, while you should always continue to grow and strive to become a better version of yourself, it is okay to relax and enjoy the moment once you accomplish your dreams. When you accomplish your dreams, you will undoubtedly experience a deep sense of fulfillment and contentment because you did not give up or you stayed focus until you made your dreams become your reality.

CHAPTER 7

What Is Your Why?

What are your dreams? Do you dream of owning your own business? Do you have a dream home in mind? Do you dream of owning a boat? Is it owning a private island? Maybe you dream of finally quitting your job. But the next question would be: Why do you want to quit your job? Is it because you want the freedom and flexibility to spend more time with your family? Do you dream of quitting your current job in favor of that dream job that you have always wanted? Is it because you want to start your own business?

If you want to quit your job so that you can start your own business, why do you want to have your own business? Is it the flexibility that it will give you? Is it that you simply want to be your own boss, or is it that you think that your own business will mean financial stability and security for you and your family? The reason why you have the dreams that you do and why you want them to come true will determine the steps that you will need to take to accomplish those dreams.

So, here is a crucial question for you: What is your why? Why do you want to accomplish the goals that you have set for yourself? What is so important about achieving your goals? Why do you even have the dream that you do? What's the big deal about this particular dream? Why is this particular dream right for you? People may see you really working hard and may admire your tenacity and how focused and dedicated you are to achieve your goals, but have you stopped to think of why you are working so hard to see your dreams come true?

You feel certain that accomplishing your dreams will make you happy, but what exactly is it about that particular dream that will make you so happy, really? Why will living your dream make you feel successful and contented with what you have accomplished? You should feel passionate about your dreams, but you should also know where that passion is coming from. Remember that vision board that I talked about in the previous chapter? That is where you should indicate your why. It is important that you understand why you are so passionate about fulfilling your dreams. You should dig deep to understand why you remain so focused and dedicated to making your dreams come true.

Your why are the reasons why accomplishing your dreams is so important to you. Your why may include gaining financial stability for yourself and your family, helping your parents retire, being able to spend more time with your family, being able to afford to send your children to college, increasing your overall self-confidence, or any other number of reasons. Your why will further serve as a source of motivation that will inspire you to keep going after your dreams when the going gets rough and you feel like giving up.

Your why will be the result of all your hard work, your tenacity and your unwavering commitment to making your dreams come true. In fact, your why should be tied in with your plan either in the form of words or on a vision board where you will be constantly reminded why you must not stop until you have accomplished your dreams. Your why are the things that will serve as constant reminders to you that you have to go out there and take your dreams if you really want them.

Since you already know that no-one will stop by and simply give your dreams to you, your why will remind you that it is up to you to go in search of them and grab those dreams with both hands once you find them. You have to hold on really tight and not let go. You have to remain focused on why you have that dream in the first place and what exactly it will mean to you and your loved ones once that dream comes true. Once you hold on to your why and not lose sight of it, it will be much easier for you to accomplish your dreams.

CHAPTER 8

Learn From The Mistakes Of Others

Now, let's talk about why we should take every opportunity we can to learn from the mistakes of others. I understand that you may have looked at the title of this chapter and thought, "Learn from the mistakes of others? No, I don't think so. I need to make and learn from my own mistakes, not from those of others." This is a misconception that many people have, but I am here to tell you that no, that is not true at all. You can and should take every opportunity to learn from the mistakes of others so that you don't make those same mistakes yourself. We should all learn from mistakes, even if those mistakes are not our own.

If you can learn from the mistakes of others, why would you not want to take that opportunity? Why would you not want to avoid making those same mistakes yourself? We all know people who have dreams, whether it is our parents, grandparents, siblings, aunts, uncles, neighbors, or friends. Whoever those people are to us, we all know people who are trying to make their dreams come true, or who have already made their dreams come true. Whether their goal is to start their own business or to go to college or to get their GED because they did not finish high school, or any other myriad of goals that they have set for themselves, you can and should take the opportunity to learn from the mistakes that they make on your way to making their dreams become their reality and ensure that you do not make those same mistakes yourself.

Oftentimes, the dreams of others are similar to our own. Even if those dreams are not exactly the same as yours, they are usually similar enough so that the person may experience stumbling blocks that are similar to the challenges that you are likely to face on your path to accomplishing your own dreams.

In trying to make his/her goals, dreams and desires come true, if that person take a wrong turn and you can identify that wrong turn for the mistake that it is, then when you experience a similar challenge on your way to accomplishing your own dreams, you will know that that turn is one that you should avoid at all costs. This is because you will already know that that going in that direction will take you off the path toward your dream. If you have a similar goal as someone else you know and you are on the same trajectory as that person, then if something did not work for that person to achieving that goal, then you can be sure that it likely will not work for you either.

This means that you should avoid taking that step yourself. You need to be smart about it by avoiding the mistakes that others made when they were trying to accomplish their dreams and so were in the shoes that you are currently wearing. As such, if you can identify those mistakes, you should definitely take the opportunity to learn from those people's mistakes and not make those same mistakes yourself while you try to achieve your own goals. To be the best version of yourself at all times, we have to learn from mistakes, whether those mistakes are our own or those of others.

If a woman got pregnant when she was in high school and had a daughter, that daughter may grow up hearing about how young her mother was when she got pregnant with her, and she may decide early on in her life that she would not make the same mistake as her mother made to become sexually active at a young age, which resulted in her pregnancy and forced her to become a high school dropout and a teenage mother. In this case, that daughter would have made a conscious decision to learn from the mistake of her mother and not to run the risk of getting pregnant herself before she is ready by choosing to not become sexually active while she is still in high school. She would have decided that she did not want teenage pregnancy to become a pattern in their family and that teenage pregnancy become an ongoing cycle that continues from one generation of the family to the next in her family.

This decision would have been easy for that daughter to make if she had the right mindset, especially if getting pregnant and dropping out of high school resulted in her mom not being able to see her dreams come true. That daughter would have then decided that she wants more for her life and that she would not make the same mistake because it could result in her jeopardizing her chance of accomplishing her own dreams.

In addition to learning from the mistakes of others, you should also study the steps that were taken by others who have already accomplished the same dream that you are trying to accomplish, especially those who were in a similar situation as the one you are currently in. What did they do to accomplish their dreams? What are some of the steps that they took on the road to their dreams?

There is no reason to reinvent the wheel when we are trying to accomplish our dreams. If we can follow the same steps that others took and implement some or all of the things that they did to achieve their goals, then we should quickly grab that opportunity with both hands and follow those steps. Whatever worked for them will likely work for you too, so do not be afraid to use their methods to achieve your own goals. If there are shortcuts that we can take when reaching for our dreams, then we should make use of the opportunity and take those shortcuts.

CHAPTER 9

Be Honest With Yourself

I know you may think that you have always been and will always be honest with yourself, but think carefully about this question before you jump to give an answer: Are you really being honest with yourself when it comes to your dreams, those goals that you have set for yourself? You see, you may have had a dream since you were a little girl and you told your parents, grandparents, siblings, cousins, friends, and everyone else who would listen that that was your dream and that is what you would become when you grow up. That idea may have been your dream for many years and so that was the goal that you set for yourself. However, believe it or not, sometimes our dreams change.

As people, we change in many different ways over time, but how we change and the extent to which we change are based on a number of factors, including our life experiences and our environment. We change as human beings as we get older and become more mature. Sometimes our dreams and ambitions also change as we get older and we find that we want something different from what we wanted when we were younger.

As we get older, we often understand more about the things we said we wanted when we were younger and, consequently, we look at things in a different light or see things from a different perspective from that which we saw them before because they became so much clearer to us after we became adults. These changes sometimes result in us changing our minds about what we want to do as a career over the course of our lifetime and who we want to become over time. In other words, our dreams sometimes change as we get older and become different people in terms of how we see the world, how we see life and how we want to live our lives.

Even though we sometimes feel this way and have a change of heart regarding our dreams as we get older, we often think that we are obligated to hang on to our old dreams for dear life! We often feel this way because we do not want to disappoint others. We may think that if we do not make every effort to accomplish our old dreams, then we will not live up to the standard that others have set for us. We feel that we must still go through with our plans to make that old dream come true because otherwise we will let down not only ourselves but also our family and friends who have been expecting us to achieve those goals that we had been telling them about all our lives. You may think that you have had that dream for such a long time and so you have to move forward with it because you cannot stop going after that dream at this late stage, or else you will be considered a failure who did not have the guts to go all the way to make that dream come true.

It is completely okay for us to let go of our old dreams and embrace new ones when we find ourselves in this situation! If you find that you no longer feel the same way about a dream that you had when you were younger and you have found that something new is your passion, your aspiration, then go after that new dream and let go of the old one. Your parents and other family members may be surprised and may even feel a little disappointed, especially if they had their minds set on that old dream of yours, but you will have a much more satisfying and rewarding life if you follow your heart and go after the new dream and let go of the old. Your aspirations and goals may change over time, and it is important for us to be honest with ourselves if this occurs and not force ourselves to go after a dream that is no longer our dream.

Sometimes it is not that our dreams have changed or that we no longer are interested in becoming what we wanted to become when we were younger. Oftentimes, as we change and become a better version of ourselves over time, we find that we now have new interests and we may decide to simply build on the old dream instead of letting it go completely. In this case, we would expand on that old dream, make it bigger and better, while not necessarily changing the dream entirely.

Regardless of the situation that you may find yourself in regarding your old dreams, new dreams, or wanting to expand on those old dreams, it is imperative that you are honest with yourself so that you can determine how best to move forward for your own inner peace, satisfaction, fulfillment and sense of accomplishment. You have to do the things that will make you happy because you cannot depend on others to do those things for you. So, if you want to have a happy life, it is up to you to do what your heart desires and grab your dreams, the ones that you have now, and stay true to yourself by doing all that you can to make them come true.

Elisa Douglas

CHAPTER 10

Don't Give Up!

Just how significant is it to you that you stay focused on the path to your dreams and not give up, regardless of the stumbling blocks that you will likely come across? In an earlier chapter, I briefly spoke about how important it is that you don't give up when you are trying to accomplish your dreams even though there will be stumbling blocks along the way. There will undoubtedly be a lot of hurdles that you will have to jump over as you reach for your dreams, but you cannot give up on those dreams because of those barriers. You have to be fully committed to accomplishing your dreams and staying the course. You have to have faith that your dreams will come true, believe in yourself and have the confidence that you can make it happen.

You may have spent years, maybe even decades, thinking about that dream and hoping that it is not too late for you to accomplish it; praying that you have what it takes to stand the test of time and stay the course until you reach that finish line and can finally live that dream. In chapter 1, I spoke about believing in yourself and believing that you can do it, that you can make your dreams come true if you are willing to put in the hard work that is required to make it happen. With belief in yourself comes a full commitment to the process and a deep desire to see it through to the end. This means that you cannot give up on your dreams regardless of the challenges that will come your way.

Giving up on one's dreams can have some detrimental effects on that person's life. It can make you feel really depressed and stressed out all the time because you will feel so very unhappy with yourself that you did not put in the work necessary to accomplish your dreams. With this will come a deep sense of shame, disappointment, anger and frustration. It can affect a person's self-esteem significantly as well and can cause a feeling of worthlessness and insignificance. You may blame yourself and think that you didn't deserve your dream anyway. There are many good people in the world who repeatedly make bad decisions, they just make too many wrong choices and at least some of them usually have harsh consequences. These wrong choices can also cause people to have a low self-esteem and can lead them to believe that their dreams would not have come through even if they had not given up because they did not deserve to live that dream anyway.

Do you want to live with regrets? Do you want to constantly wonder of what your life would have been like eventually had you not given up on your dreams? Do you want to live a life where you constantly question whether you had given your dreams your all and really did everything you could to make those dreams come true? Here is where you have to be honest with yourself again. You have to make sure that you've pushed yourself 110% at each step along the way to accomplishing your dreams.

Dreams are not meant to stay as dreams forever; that's not how this works. You are actually supposed to go out there and do what you have to do to make your dreams become your reality. As I said in an earlier chapter, it is okay for your dream to seem improbable when it is first conceived. You may think initially that there is little chance that your dream will actually come true, but you have to believe in the possibility of your dream enough so that you will be motivated to put in the work that is necessary to make it come true. Do not mistakenly think that your dreams are impossible just because you realize that they will be difficult to accomplish. Difficulty and impossibility are two very different things.

Oftentimes, we give up on our dreams just before that big break that we were hoping for. That stumbling block that was in the way when we gave up was probably the last one that we would have come across and our dream was right there on the other side of that block. We just needed to stay the course for just a little while longer. This is why I am imploring you to keep the faith and believe that if you continue to work toward your dreams, pushing constantly toward them at a steady pace, that those dreams will eventually come true. There will be challenging times, yes, but you have to be resilient and remain vigilant. The saying is so true: Good things come to those who wait! Patience, resilience and hard work are the keys to making our dreams come true!

So, what are some other things that are likely to happen if you decide to give up on your dreams? Chronic stress that is caused by the disappointment of not fulfilling your dreams can further result in chronic diseases such as hypertension and diabetes. Overweight or obesity can also be a side effect of giving up on our dreams. This is because when we give up on our dreams, as women, many of us will develop the habit of over-eating because we feel depressed and we are in constant distress which, of course, then leads to us becoming overweight.

When we give up on our dreams, we often become miserable and quite difficult to be around. You may find yourself complaining a lot about your life or about your environment and may become really overbearing. This may result in you inadvertently pushing your friends and even family members away and you may find that they start keep their distance from you because they are no longer comfortable being around you. They may feel like you have become toxic to their peace of mind.

When you reach your 70s and 80s, the regret of giving up your dreams will be stronger than ever because this is the age range when human beings really start examining their life choices and start thinking about how they could have made their lives better by living a more meaningful life. You may worry that you are almost at the age of retirement and still haven't accomplished the dreams that you had when you were a teenager even though over the years those dreams did not ever change or waver. However, it is extremely important to remember that it is never too late to accomplish your dreams, so you cannot (you absolutely cannot!) give up and use your age as an excuse to not follow those dreams.

When you fall short of reaching your dreams because you gave up on them before they came true, do not blame your environment, your situation or the people around you, as many of us are prone to do. To ensure that you do not fall into the trap of playing the blame game regarding why you did not accomplish your dreams, you just need to stick to the plan that you put in place when your dream was born. You will be full of regrets if you don't, so you have to make a conscious decision to be resilient so that when those hurdles come in your way, you will not hesitate to jump over them so you can continue your journey toward your dreams.

There are usually several different 'roads' that you can take to accomplishing your dreams, so if you find that one road is blocked and there is no way through it, then you just have to find another 'road' that is open and clear to get you to your final destination where you reach your dreams. Despite the obstacles that will come in your path, you have to jump over them or walk around them, then you pick yourself up, dust yourself off, and keep it moving toward your dream.

Giving up on your dreams means that you will not be able to live the rewarding and fulfilling life that you always wanted and you will not get the chance to experience the benefits of living your dreams like you have always envisioned for yourself. Following your passion and staying committed to your cause will play a big role in whether or not you succeed. In this case, your actions should most certainly speak louder than your words. Of course, as we go through life, we will all experience failure from time to time because we cannot always win. However, it is important that we learn to accept failure and adapt to new situations and circumstances when we come across them. On the other hand, we should never compromise on our values and principles because those are what make us who we are and without them, we will not be our most authentic selves.

It is really not difficult to follow your dreams. Many people think that it is almost impossible for a person to make all their dreams come true, but that is definitely not the case. Despite the many obstacles and roadblocks that come hand-in-hand with going after our dreams, having a solid plan, the right mindset and faith in God can make those obstacles seem like only minor annoyances. Our dreams will not only impact us, but they will also have an impact on the people in our lives. However, this impact should be positive all around, assuming that your dream has nothing to do with anything illegal or unethical. Something that can only be accomplished through illegal or unethical means should definitely never become anyone's dream.

Some people follow their dreams relentlessly and do all they can to make them come true because they want to motivate their children by showing them that they can accomplish anything that they set their minds to. In an effort to inspire their children, these individuals see their children as their why, their reason for accomplishing their dreams. In chapter 5, I spoke about how my mom inspired my siblings and I to go after our dreams and to not give up on them, not matter the disappointments, obstacles and drawbacks that we may experience along the way. Even though she became a midwife before she started having children, her story still served as a huge source of inspiration to us, although we did not actually live through that experience with her.

Sometimes we also have to make a conscious decision to start putting ourselves first when we really want to make our dreams come through. It's not about being selfish or caring only for ourselves; it is about making a decision that we deserve to be happy and contented too. It is about staying true to who we are so that we do not become only what others want us to be, instead of what we want for ourselves. It is about seeing our value and our potential and believing that we what it takes to make our dreams come true. The support of family and friends is also great, but you have to believe in yourself to make your dreams come true, with or without the support of others. It is about wanting a better life for yourself and your family.

There are many reasons why people give up on their dreams and these reasons often vary from one person to the next, depending on personality, mindset, faith in a higher power, and discipline. One of the primary reasons why people give up on their dreams is because they do not have the right mindset and they give up on themselves when the going gets rough. They lose faith in the process; they stop believing in themselves and in their ability to do whatever it takes to make their dreams come true. These people often lack the confidence, discipline, commitment, resilience and faith in God that are all necessary for them to accomplish their dreams. Hope goes together with our faith and you will also need hope in spades when going after your dreams. Our dreams were not meant to come by easily; they are the things that we must work very hard for so that we can someday live those dreams.

You must have the tenacity that is required to see your journey to the end where your dreams inevitably will be if you maintain the qualities that are necessary for you to make it to the end. Ask any successful people you know, and they will tell you that you need all these qualities in spades to become successful in anything you endeavor to do. Even if you saw people quitting all around you when you were growing up, that is not the way to go or the way to accomplish anything in life, so do not be a quitter. However, it takes a lot of guts to stay true to your purpose, and this is why it is imperative that you truly believe in yourself, trust the process, have a solid plan in place and never, ever give up before you get to that final destination where you are living your dreams!

CHAPTER 11

It's Not Too Late!

It is never too late to follow your dreams! Let me repeat that. It is never, ever too late to follow your dreams! Now, you may think that I am crazy for saying that because all your life you may have dreamed of going to college and earning your bachelor's degree, but it never happened for you. Now you are retired, and your grandchildren are about to start college. Let me tell you something: It is not too late for you and you can start college too!

When I was in college, I took classes with many students who were old enough to be my grandparents. I was so fascinated that these adults wanted to actually sit in a class with us "kids" at the time, study with us and do projects with us and I asked many of them why they decided to go to college at this "late hour of the day", so to speak. After most of these conversations, I would look at these amazing individuals very differently, with so much respect and admiration for their strength, courage and their absolute refusal to give up on their dreams! Their stories helped me to understand their drive and their courage in actually being brave and determined enough to decide that they would earn their college degrees, no matter what!

At the end of each school year, during graduation season, we also hear many stories on television about extraordinarily brave men and women who pushed the envelope despite their advanced ages and believed in themselves enough to go after their dreams. These people are heroes in my book, because heroism to me is all about being brave and courageous enough to do something that seems highly improbable or even impossible to others. It is the drive that is at the core of many of us that keeps us going in times of deep struggle and distress.

I gave the example of the many elderly people who I went to college with to say this: It is never too late to accomplish your dreams! As long as you have life and you still have that fire in your belly, you can go out there and make your dreams come true. Do not let anyone talk you out of seeing your dreams become your reality. Do not let them tell you that you can't do it, that you are too old, that you have too many other things going on in your life to go after your dreams. If you want that dream badly enough, you will find the time and energy and put in the hard work that is required to make it happen. You will find the time to be persistent enough to not stop going until that dream becomes your reality and you are living the life that you have always dreamed of!

Elisa Douglas

CONCLUSION

You need to be mindful of your dreams, keep your focus on them, and have a solid plan of action of how you will make those dreams come true. You have to want your dreams so badly, you should be so hungry for them, that you will not see failure as an option and you will not give up on those dreams, no matter the challenges that you face as you work hard to make them come true. As you work toward fulfilling your dreams, it is imperative that you keep your why at the forefront of your mind. Why are your dreams so important to you? Why are so working so hard to make them come true? How will your life change when your dreams finally come true? What is the impact that living your dream will have on your family and other loved ones?

Believe in God and put your trust in Him and He will guide and direct you on your path to seeing your dreams come true. Be mindful, be disciplined, be committed, be humble, be patient, be persistent, be resilient, and your dreams will certainly come true.

Never let the naysayers get in your way of fulfilling your dreams. Those people who are always discouraging you. The ones who are always telling you that you cannot do it, that you are wasting your time, money and energy chasing after something imaginary, that you should get real and start focusing on more realistic goals. These naysayers are oftentimes the same ones who are quick to jump back on your bandwagon, so to speak, when you accomplish your dreams. Do not let them discourage you and talk you into giving up on your dreams. You have to believe in yourself 100%. You have to trust that you know what you are doing and that you have the ability to get it done.

Despite the stumbling blocks that will come in your way as you reach for your dreams, step over them, push them out of your way, or if they are too much to handle, then take another route to get to your dreams. Whatever it is that you have to do, do it for yourself because you deserve to live the life that you want. Do it because when you fulfill your dreams, you will feel a sense of accomplishment that you have never felt before. You will feel a deep sense of self-worth and your confidence level will go through the roof! You will feel like you are on top of the world and that is when you will truly feel happy and contented and will be able to live your best and most fulfilling life. Accomplishing your dreams will make you a much better human being who will love life because you will have become the very best version of yourself!

To further recap, remember that a written plan of how you will accomplish your dreams that is implemented and closely followed can help you achieve your goals much faster. Without a plan to guide you from point A to point Z, the journey to accomplishing your dreams will be much more painful because you will likely make a lot of unnecessary mistakes along the way. It is also very important that you are honest with yourself and change your path if your dreams change along the way. Learn from the mistakes of others, especially those who also had the same dreams as you do and have already seen those dreams come true for themselves.

By studying the steps that these individuals took to accomplish their dreams, you can learn from their mistakes and avoid making them yourself, which will save you a lot of time, energy, and in most cases, even money. Furthermore, following a path that is similar to the one that these individuals took to achieve their goals will also ensure that you accomplish your dreams much faster than you would have if you had used the trial and error method on your own journey toward your dreams.

I will end with my favorite saying: Whatever the mind can conceive, it can achieve! I truly believe that whatever it is that you put your mind to, you can achieve it! So, keep going forward toward your dreams and do not get distracted. Stay on the path to your success and to living your best life ever! Write your dreams down on paper or put them on a vision board and remind yourself of them daily. Now…go get it! You got this, girl! I believe in you because I know for sure that you have what it takes to make it happen. I'm rooting for you! Now go and make that dream of yours become your reality!

Girl, Don't Stop Dreaming

About the Author

Elisa Douglas is a public health educator, health and wellness coach, and motivational speaker who focuses on motivating others to reach their full potential.

She also enjoys sharing her experiences with others who can then apply those experiences to improving one or more aspects of their own lives. She has been inspired by many people in her life over the years who have shown her that anything is possible if you believe.

In her books for women, she shares inspirational stories and words of wisdom based on her own experiences. The aim of her books is to uplift, motivate and inspire women all over the world to use their power and resilience to create the happy and rewarding life they deserve!

Elisa lives in New Jersey with her family.

Girl, Don't Stop Dreaming

www.ingramcontent.com/pod-product-compliance
Lightning Source LLC
Chambersburg PA
CBHW031601040426
42452CB00006B/373